Survival:
The Voyage of
"Yacht Black Jed"

Zan Swartzberg

DEDICATION

For Lorraine and Peter,
Yacht Red Ruth
With affection and admiration.

CONTENTS

ACKNOWLEDGMENTS

My thanks to my wife Noreen, for encouraging me to write this story. My admiration and heartfelt thanks to the wonderful Skipper and crew of Black Jed.

Skipper: Andrew Jackson

Crew: Stephen Sykes
Gary Becker
Graham Rouke
Sheralee Williams
Debbie McDonald
Paul Dugmore

1 HOW IT BEGAN

I was born in a sleepy little hamlet in the heart of the Orange Free State in South Africa. My parents were immigrants from Lithuania and Egypt who travelled far and wide before arriving in South Africa. Their travels were necessary events of survival in the evasion of pogroms that had been implemented in the countries in which they lived.

My father travelled to London where he worked for a few years before travelling on to South Africa. During his business life he and my mother would travel extensively.

I believe that one of my inherited genetic paths was to be a desire for adventure and travel.

During my formative years, my best friend in the village was Ray Meyer. Our friendship continued for over seventy years and we had many adventures.

Living in Bethlehem in the 1950's an application by my brother and I to join the local Yacht and Speed Boat Club was denied, we believe, due to our religious affiliation. Anti-Semitism was part of life back then. As a result, and because we so desperately wanted to sail and in freedom, without prejudice, we founded the Athlone Yacht Club.

Ray was working as a pharmacist in Durban in the 1980's, and as was his custom, on Friday afternoons he met with his colleagues at the Royal Natal Yacht Club for a drink and a natter.

I often reminded Ray that one of my ambitions was to crew on a yacht from South Africa to Europe and he should keep his eye focused on the bulletin board for any notices by skippers looking for crew.

One evening, early in March 1983, I received a 'phone call from Ray. "Zan, if you are still interested in this 'meshugga' (crazy) yacht trip, contact Andrew Jackson at the Mercedes factory in East London".

This I did post haste. Andrew was due to represent his company at the Rand Easter Show in Johannesburg in April and we arranged to meet for an interview.

After the usual third-degree questions as to my sailing experience and physical capabilities, he proceeded to enlighten me as to the ever-present uncertainties of a hazardous voyage.

A very important consideration was the fact that one would be cooped up with six other individuals, all disparate in customs, temperaments and personalities. The range included charming, agreeable, good humoured and, depending on the weather, perverse, obstinate, uncooperative and stubborn. An insensitive remark could result in a psychopathic eruption of a character into a complete opposite to normal behaviour.

"Do you have the right attitude to cope with it?"

The safety of the whole operation depends on everyone pulling together as a team regardless of personality clashes.

Andy warned that if this happened in the early days of a three-month cruise then heaven help us! Andy had sailed and crewed for many years and knew, from experience, what he was talking about.

His projections came true to a certain degree and fortunately only toward the end of our expedition.

2 TRAIN JOURNEY

I was due to rendezvous with Andy in East London on 25th April 1983. My travel arrangements were to take the train from to Bloemfontein. There I would change to the train to Grahamstown where I would stay a few days with my friends Gerhard and Maggie von Hasseln. They were game and cattle ranchers in the district who took wealthy tourists on shooting expeditions. They would then take me by car to East London via Port Elizabeth.

I had booked a first-class berth for the Bloemfontein to Grahamstown part of the journey. When I arrived at my compartment at about nine o'clock in the evening, I was rather taken aback by the sight of an unkempt looking individual snoring his head off on the bottom bunk. He was dressed in a grubby T-shirt, shabby creased denims and wearing slipslops on his feet.

I thought to myself, "How the heck am I going to get this hobo out of the compartment?"

I settled down for a read and a snack of sandwiches. As the train pulled out of the station my travelling companion woke up. I have learnt by experience through my many years of roaming; never but never judge a person by his appearance.

I immediately extended my hand in greeting and offered him a sandwich and a swig from my hip flask.

The young man proved to be in his late twenties, surprisingly fluent in both English and Afrikaans and quite talkative. If he was on the popular radio show "What's my Line", I doubt if the team would guess what his profession was. After a few quaffs of the malt and to justify his appearance, his tongue went into overdrive.

He was attached to the Diamond branch of the South African Police Force. His father was a brigadier, very highly ranked in the force, and he was in this job dealing with huge amounts of money in questionable assignments due to his family connections.

His background credentials had to be impeccable. He was required to frequent pubs in hotels and city saloons, shebeens and night clubs. He was to seek out likely, well dressed and affluent candidates. Approach them, in a seemingly inebriated state, and offer to sell them illegal diamonds at ridiculously low prices. To justify his credentials with his willing prospects, he would whip out of his wallet various identity documents issued by De Beers Mining Company. These would show that he was an employee of the company in their operation to retrieve diamonds from the seabed off the Namibian Skeleton Coast. Others, that he was in the classification division grading the stones, or that he was chief of security and so forth. To all intent and purposes, he would prove that he had easy access to obtaining unlimited supplies of illicit stock for disposing of 'under the counter'. The Identity cards were genuine. The diamond and gold mining companies were working with the government to take extreme measures to put a stop to IDB and IGB (Illegal Diamond Buying and Illegal Gold Buying), which was causing millions in losses to the mining houses and a loss of tax revenue to the Government.

The next stage of the sting was to invite the prospective buyer up to his hotel suite and show them the merchandise. Then they would both settle on a purchase price with an appointment made to meet to make the exchange. The operator would inform his handler of the details and as the exchange was made a team of detectives would pounce and make the necessary arrests. These cases were highly publicized as a means to discourage other get-rich quick wheeler dealers.

He told me of one occasion where it went hopelessly wrong. The police lost the cash and the parcel of diamonds and the buyer got away with it due to lack of evidence. I have my own private thoughts on what happened. Perhaps a reverse 'sting' and the buyer had made a pact with the 'seller' and they are both enjoying life with a numbered Swiss bank account paying interest regularly? By the nature of this young man's vocation his working life was numbered and eventually a contract on his life would likely be taken out.

As the train trundled along the young man produced from under the bunk a briefcase, much like those in James Bond movies. He twirled the combination lock and opened the lid to show me the contents. There, in neat little compartments and graded according to size and colour, lay hundreds of the most beautiful uncut diamonds. He asked me to guess the value. "One million", I said. "Double it would be closer", he remarked.

On arrival at Grahamstown station Maggie and Gerhard were waiting to meet me. I spent a few pleasant days with them on their farm, 'Thornbush'.

When it was time to leave, Gerhard shot a buck and Maggie prepared it for the pot. I was to take it with me to the crew as our fresh rations for the first part of the sail down south.

We left Thornbush and drove in their four-wheel drive Landcruiser to East London. The yacht was moored at the Irvin & Johnson private docks on the Buffalo river. It wasn't an easy location to find, but eventually I came face to face with my new home for the next few months.

3 YACHT BLACK JED

The yacht was classed as a Cruiser/racer yacht. It had all the modern conveniences to make living a more comfortable affair. At the same time, for racing purposes, she had a fair turn of speed. She was a Monte Video 43 class yacht. She was 43 feet in length and 15 feet wide with a 60-foot black anodized mast. The keel was weighted with 10 tons of lead, so she was extremely stable with little chance of 'turning turtle'. In the event that this did happen she would right herself without fuss or bother.

She had a full wardrobe of North manufactured sails. 3 jib sails of different sizes including a large Genoa sail. The Main sail and two Spinnakers and a storm jib were included in the sail locker.

A small tender (colloquially nominated as a Rubber Duck) with a small outboard motor for ship to shore and yacht to yacht visits. For cold comfort a life raft was stowed aft for easy launching.

When we arrived at the dock there was no-one in sight and I invited Maggie and Gerhard to come aboard and inspect the cabins with me. We were astounded at the beautiful workmanship of the furnishings and the elegance of the lounge upholstery, covered in quality pastel wine coloured velvet.

4 NEIGHBOURS

The only other vessel in the quay was moored about ten metres away. Yacht "Kya Lami" was flying a Port Natal Yacht Club burgee from the stern. This was a huge yacht of ferro cement construction. A framework of steel reinforcing shaped to the design of the hull is formed, then a concrete mixture is sprayed onto the steel to complete the skin structure. Because of the economic cost and easy method of manufacture, many home builders used this method for their own construction. One problem was that the whole hull required to be sprayed in one operation for a faultless curing, otherwise cracks would develop later with disastrous results.

Whilst working on our boat we would occasionally catch a glimpse of the Zulu crewman who lived on board Kya Lami. He was obviously there to look after things for the absent owner. One morning at the crack of dawn, Andy came below to wake us up. He asked if we had heard anything untoward during the night.

Graham Rouke, Andy and I were the only ones on board at that time and neither of us had heard anything.

The news was that Kya Lami had sunk at its moorings during the night. There was no sign of the crewman and we wondered whether he had gone down with the craft. We reported this to the port captain and heard nothing further until the day we were about to cast off. Two important looking individuals arrived at our mooring requesting permission to come aboard. They introduced themselves as representatives from the insurance company. They wished to interrogate us with regard to the suspicious circumstances in which yacht Kya Lami had foundered We were always sceptical as to the sea-worthiness of the vessel considering the rust marks emanating from the many fine hair-line cracks in the hull and we got the impression that the assessors believed it had been deliberately scuttled. A hefty claim had been lodged with them.

It is a well-known fact that ferro cement yachts were very difficult to sail, for many reasons. One being the extremely heavy hull resulting in sluggish performance.

Unfortunately, we could be of no assistance to them.

The owner of Yacht Kya Lami alleged in his insurance claim that the gas tank used with the cooking apparatus had exploded, gutting the interior, rupturing the structure and resulting in the sinking. None of us had heard any sound of the explosion or the roaring of the flames. We certainly were not so stoned that none of us heard anything unusual and blissfully slept peacefully through it all!

5 PORT ELIZABETH TO CAPE TOWN

Logbook notes

Our voyage of Yacht Black Jed is a tribute to our skipper, Andrew (Andy) Jackson. Only fully qualified Skippers with deep sea ratings are permitted to captain keeled boats. Safety regulations galore apply.

May 1st, 1983

14h00: Home Port East London.

We motor slowly out of our berth and down the Buffalo River on a beautiful day. Crossing the booms, we are at last out into the open, if choppy, sea.

We pick up a light north easterly wind of 10 to 15 knots. Barometer reading 1009. Clearance given from the harbour master and our course is set to 240 degrees, heading for Port Elizabeth.

Sails fully up with a light weight number 1 main sail.

Crew on board: Skipper Andy Jackson, Gary Becker, Graham Rouke, Stephen Sykes, Sheralee Williams and Zan Swartzberg.

Two crew members will join us in Cape Town; Debbie McDonald and Paul Dugmore.

Sheralee works for Wilson Rowntree sweet factory and brought with her a generous supply of assorted sweets and chocolates, donated by her colleagues.

15h00: Andy gets the feel of handling Black Jed. He decides the wind is blowing just right and gives us rookies the first lesson in hoisting the Spinnaker. It's a tricky operation for first time amateurs, especially trimming the huge billowing sail. It was blowing all over the show like a playful delinquent kite. Celebratory drinks on the captain. With the motion of the seas and the alcohol, a nice mix for that woozy feeling!

18h00: Stephen, being an old hand at this sailing business, offers to prepare supper. Pickles with snack biscuits for starters and Maggie's venison, with a selection of canned veggies. Canned fruit salad and cheese to follow. We all have ravenous appetites, courtesy of sea breezes and elation.

22h00: Wind gusting to 25 knots, force 5, South West. Hey man, things are getting rough. Andy at the helm as we pass the Fish River lights on our starboard.

24h00: Magic hour of midnight. The moon peeps out from behind scattered clouds. I look up at the navigation lights mounted high up on the main mast. Big mistake! Swaying against the cloudy background disorientated my balance and left me dizzy and nauseous. I am as sick as a dog and feed the fish with Maggie's delicious venison.

Not wasted I suppose but a small consolation.

May 2nd, 1983

02h00: Kenton on our starboard. Wind gusting 40 knots. Logged 265 nautical miles since leaving East London. The motion is fierce. We are coasting along at a fiery rate of knots. Bird Island is abeam.

15h00: Arrived Port Elizabeth and berthed next to Yacht "Sitatunga". Head off to the Yacht club for a shower and shave. Port Elizabeth – the friendly city.

To catch up on the latest news I bought the local newspaper. What a coincidence as I read a long article about my old friend Wim Klapwijk, who now lives in Mossel Bay, which is our next port of call. He and I were founder members of the Athlone Yacht Club in Bethlehem, way back in 1951. Wim emigrated from Holland and set up business operating bulldozers, donga bashing and building farm dams. He left Bethlehem to go pineapple farming in East London where he made a fortune laying pipe for the Mossel Bay municipality. According to the newspaper article he was now taking tourists out on his home-built yacht, from the harbour to Seal Island. I remember doing this trip two years ago, but I didn't even recognize him. I recalled that I had been annoyed with the skippers' devilish sense of humour, close hauling the boat to the wind and showering all the passengers with sea spray. It ruined by Leica camera. I think maybe it's payback time!

May 3rd, 1983

09h00: Cleared the port. Jib and Jenny drawing like an old smoke stack. Andy gives instruction to hoist the spinnaker bag. Black Jed surfing along majestically at ten knots. It's exhilarating. The crew are content, and a delicious brunch served. Andy is experimenting with the self-steering device. It has been out of operation for many moons. The spray dodger is deflecting the wind and spray from the cockpit, doing its job and working overtime.

May 5th, 1983

Cape seals in abundance. Knysna on our starboard and vanishing into the distance. The man on lookout spotted, too late, a large area of dense kelp, floating half submerged ahead of us. Despite taking evasive action we plow on with disastrous consequences. Black Jed staggers to a halt. Panic stations! Willing hands hoist down all canvas. Although our sails are manufactured from hi-tech Teflon which is light weight, quick dry, resilient and durable, the old expressions die hard, and sails are still referred to as canvas.

Graham goes overboard to remove the seaweed snagged on the keel and propeller.

12h00: Zan helming. Sails are down and we are motoring. Within an hour we will be in Mossel Bay.

12h45: Andy on the radio to port captain requesting permission to enter the harbour. Now we have heard everything as the Captain replies, "Sorry I'm off to lunch. Come back at 2pm". What a bloody chutzpa!

15h00: Safely berthed and tucked up for the night. Andy considers putting in a complaint about port rules. Imagine visiting yachtsmen from the United States and elsewhere having to put up with this bureaucratic nonsense. He decided otherwise as the port authorities may get nasty and decide to inspect our boat, finding something trivial to use in refusing to let us leave. Andy decided he might do it later.

For the rest of the afternoon all able-bodied men lug our ten 50 litre heavy duty plastic containers the half mile to the Shell depot to top up with diesel. It is back breaking work. Decks are swabbed and ropes neatly coiled leaving everything ship shape and in apple pie order. Hopefully we'll be getting a visit from Wim and we want to impress him.

We didn't know it at the time, but whilst we were cruising around in circles waiting to enter the port, Wim was in his hill top home, high above the harbour, and had his binoculars focused on us. At the time we were just another set of sails on the horizon and he thought to himself, "what the hell is that skipper up to, sailing around in dizzy circles?" This was now one of Wim's pleasures in life; watching the boating scene from his elevated eagle's nest.

4th May 1983.

Early breakfast. All crew walk to town to stretch our sea legs. On enquiry, everybody knows Wim Klapwijk. I tried to telephone him but nobody home. There are many interesting tourist attractions in a 360-year-old town. The Vasco da Gama post tree, where sailors of yore left their mail to be picked up by ships going in the opposite direction, and a fascinating nautical museum.

15h00: I finally managed to raise Wim on the phone. There was great excitement and he could not believe his ears. He hurried down to the harbour and I did the introductions. On his invitation we went back to his home to meet Marty, his wife. Use of his guest bathroom for lovely hot showers and a wonderful meal with Dutch croquettes. We reminisced about old times and for two pins, if he had no other commitments, he would have come with us. He was very envious as it was his great ambition to do such a trip. We had a delightful evening, and everybody was sloshed.

6th May 1983

06h00: We depart Mossel Bay rather late. The sun is already high in the heavens. Let's blame it all on Klapwijk. We went through the usual routine with a fresh breeze and a full working jib. We put three reefs in the main sail as this coastline is living up to its reputation of seas coming in from all directions. We can see sheet lightening miles ahead. Its cloudy, sunny, cloudy. I wish the weather would make up its mind. Just like a female! No doubt I'll be shot down in flames for that remark.

15h00: Cape Baracuta is visible through the mist on our starboard. Our chart shows the next cape to come up will be Cape Infanta. I would certainly like to know the origins of these enchanting names. "Infanta" is certainly of Portuguese extraction. Perhaps some famous Navigator?

17h00: Cape Infanta

20h00: We are now into the sheet lightening domain. In between flashes it is blacker than black.

23h00: Gary, at this late hour, suddenly pipes up; "By the way guys, today is my birthday". Legitimate justification for another drink. Gary and Sheralee finish watch on a high celebratory note.

7th May 1983

22h00: A magical moment. Coming in from Mossel Bay and cruising along the Cape coast with the Oudekraal shoreline on our starboard and approximately one hour to our destination at the yacht moorings of the Royal Cape Yacht Club in Cape Town. We pass Oudekraal, then along the esplanade to Llandudno, Bantry Bay, Clifton, Cape Point and Sea Point. We can clearly see the road traffic with the headlights like a string of pearls along the base of the berg, directly under Lions Head.

And then suddenly, out of the blue, a magnificent view of Table Mountain, floodlit by powerful electric beams, highlighting the traditional tablecloth in shimmering white, shrouding the uppermost level of the most famous view in the world.

The magic hour of midnight is ticking closer and, in a light following wind, our spinnaker sail billowing, a bright moon creeping through the shrouds of ropes, halyards, main sheets and all fascinating paraphernalia of a working boat, I wished I could freeze the moment for all time.

Quietly we cruised in, looking for the beacon lights to guide us to the yacht basin, which would protect us and all yachties from the terrible south-easter which could spring up suddenly without warning.

After dropping every stitch of sail our small inboard motor took over and motivated us into our berth. Making a few wrong turns along the way, a lone fisherman in his small dinghy guided us casually, as if this was an everyday occurrence. "Turn left at the pier, then right at the jetty, and then straight ahead until you see the sign No Parking. Then you're home".

The usual "bitter to the end" drinkers in the pub overlooking the yacht basin casually hoisted their drinks and unsteadily staggered down to seal level. An unofficial welcoming committee taking details of the latest arrival.

The normal questions began;
"Who's your skipper? Where are you from? Where are you registered? Where are you heading for? Hm, a girl on the crew? Unusual?"

Whilst being moored at the Royal Cape Yacht Club, we were continually visited by various merchants from the city, canvassing for business. This port is home to thousands of yachtsmen from all over the world, so it was big business for the ship chandlers. Traders who specialized in supplying the various branches of marine life, notable to the huge ocean passenger liners and merchant shipping. Not to mention the fishing fleets, which did their own canning on board. Taiwanese, Korean, Japanese, from well beyond our territorial waters and plundering our rich fishing grounds.

The usual procedure when coming into Port and then leaving for foreign destinations is that the skipper collects all crew passports and hands them to the Port Captain for processing. The yacht would obtain a permit to purchase liquor directly from the wholesale merchants without paying VAT and Excise Duty. These supplies would be brought on board and stowed in a secure locker by one of the Port Captains officials, and the lock would then be officially sealed. When the vessel is ten kilometres out to see, we are allowed to break the seal and uncork the first bottle of bubbly to celebrate our license to alcoholic poisoning. Crews seldom waited the mandatory ten kilometres. Who was to know?

We estimated that we would be at sea for three months. By rule of thumb, a bottle of whisky a day. That makes 90 bottles. To be on the safe side, for medicinal purposes, add another 22 bottles. And for bartering purposes, another 22 bottles. That's 11 cases. That's not a good number, let's add another dozen in case some of it goes flat! An even 12 cases of Bells nectar.

To fill in, after all, we may need an extra bit of ballast in rough weather, 5 cases of Nederburg Stein, 2 cases of Vodka, a case of Sherry (for the appetite) and for a chaser (as an afterthought) 30 cases of Castle Lager. A bottle of whisky, at retail prices, cost only R6 a bottle. Buying it wholesale and without excise duty we were paying R3 a bottle. Absolutely no need to confiscate a tot measure from the Yacht Club pub to eke it out.

6 CAPE TOWN TO ST. HELENA

Logbook notes
15th May 1983

11h00: Motor out of harbour. Many goodbyes. Friends and relatives of the crew who have come down to see us off. Also, a last minute farewell from Taffy Evans, the owner of Black Jed. With a name like that he could only be a Welshman.

Taffy first came to South Africa as a member of the British Lions Rugby Team five years previously. He decided to settle in South Africa and made his fortune as a Civil Engineer. He bought Yacht Black Jed as a means of getting his money out of the country. We were ferrying the yacht to Europe where it would be used for charter work and then for sale for hard currency.

On departure, Taffy presented the crew with T-shirts and some of the lucky ones also got woolen pullovers. Shrewd chap Taffy. On the eve of our leaving he invited the whole crew to have dinner with him at one of the fancy restaurants on the Peninsula. It ended in the small hours of the morning. It also ended by the crew not only paying for his own meal, but also paying for Taffy's meal. Not fair on Sheralee and Debbie who were travelling on a shoe string.

We also met in Cape Town a friend of Taffy's, by the name of Fritz. A millionaire spending the money he obtained after selling his factory. He made high speed inflatable boats (Rubber Ducks). Most of his production was sold to the South African Navy which was a very lucrative contract. He was building a 100-foot super deluxe cruising yacht, to be used for chartering to wealthy Americans in the Caribbean. Some of its features included three super deluxe state rooms with en suite bathrooms, Captain and crew quarters, walk-in cold room and freezer to match, the most up to date navigational equipment with satellite tracking and commercial and amateur radio equipment. The hull was in the latest hi-tech space age honeycomb fibreglass. The Captains bridge with a perfect view, a lounge for the passengers, a full wardrobe of sails and two twin six-cylinder Volvo marine diesel engines.

Fritz proudly gave Black Jed's crew a cook's tour of the work in progress, housed in a huge warehouse in one of the suburbs of Cape Town. The cost of the project 5 million Rand. A phenomenal amount in 1983.

Fritz was very gregarious and friendly and, a few days before we sailed, invited us over to his mansion in Llandudno for a going away party. No expense spared. Liquor for Africa, and Fritz, who fancied himself as a bit of a cook, supervised the mutton on a revolving spit in his state-of-the-art kitchen.

Smack in the middle of his lounge was a king size jacuzzi. By midnight the soiree was getting into its stride and the guests, including our crew, were well and truly oiled. Without inhibitions (I think this was quite the norm in Cape Town's high society) the guests were stripping down to their birthday suits to sober up in the overworked Jacuzzi. It was quite a novelty in those days to have a Jacuzzi.

15th May 1983

On our way at last. Our course is set for the Island of St. Helena in the South Atlantic. As the crow flies, a distance of 2500 kilometres. If the winds are fickle the distance could increase to 3500 kilometres. We will be tacking our way north (zig zag sailing). It makes for a very bumpy ride across a very choppy ocean. The course is 360 degrees and we have our number one jib and main sheet at full stretch. The wind is blowing 15 knots north west, barometer reading 1013. Notated; very confused sea.

16h00: made our first tack. Compass reading 300 degrees. Wind speed 20 knots westerly.

16th May 1983

Checked log for the previous day. Made 196 nautical miles. Our log is an instrument with a nylon line which is affixed to the transom. Whilst being dragged through the water the vane at the end turns with the motion and records the distance travelled during a 24 hour period.

Our distance is not satisfactory. It's ok if you are pleasure cruising but Andy is pushing hard. We continually change the sheets to get the most out of the prevailing weather conditions. Hard work for landlubbers. Our Skipper is complaining. "Where are the trade winds we have been hearing so much about?"

In Cape Town we had lots and lots of advice from experienced Skippers. Some said it was too late in the year to leave, other said it was too early. Who do you believe? There are many theories as to the joys and pleasures of hitching a ride with trade winds blowing steady and true for thousands of kilometres.

12h00: We pick up the BBC pips for the noon time check and Andy teaches Graham how to take a sighting with the sextant. Seas coming in from all directions. Difficult to keep balance, which is essential for an accurate reading. Not much to report. Crew all together for breakfast. Envy the Christians!

No hang ups about strict dietary laws. That delicious aroma of crisp fried bacon and eggs. Enough to drive a Yid's taste buds crazy. After breakfast I do my chores and the washing up. Salt water tap for the rough stuff. Go easy on the fresh water tap for rinsing. It's a small galley so everything has its place. Swept the floor, made up my bunk. Gave the head (toilet) a thorough scrub deep down. Gary and Sheralee on watch. The rest of the crew going about their personal business. I check the library and selected "By the Rivers of Babylon". Curl up on one of the hard wooden bunks lining the cockpit topsides. Did more dozing than reading. That's what the continual motion of the boat does to one's metabolism. Limp and listless most of the time.

17th May 1983

06h00: Checked log for past 24 hours. 226 nautical miles. Skippers nagging paid off with a slight improvement. Heading 340 degrees, Barometer 1018. Anemometer confirms wind gusting 20 to 25 knots. Radio call from Taffy. Interested in how Black Jed is performing. South African radio stations still coming in with strong signals. Weather reports helpful. A bit of a disturbing forecast for the next few days. GALE WARNING to all shipping on the west coast. That's us! The trade winds have arrived.

We are cruising along at a steady 10 knots. The bow slicing into the surf. The deck at a constant angle of about 15 degrees. We noticed at this steady speed and angle, a whistling sound in the rigging of the vessel. A continuous, long steady high pitch. Quite pleasant actually, and from now on our friend "Whistling Jack" joins the crew.

09h00: Out at sea the fresh sea breezes stimulate the saliva glands and generate a hearty appetite. The usual fare is served for breakfast, oranges or canned fruit to start with. A multitude of cereals, long life mild and the daily crisp fried bacon and eggs served with home baked "beer bread". Beer bread was Gary's specialty. Instead of using yeast he used a bottle of beer. The malt in the beer having the same effect as yeast. We had fresh bread on board every day. It had a bit of a beery taste to it, but we soon got used to the distinctive aroma and it was delicious toasted and eaten with marmalade and coffee.

For these past weeks since coming on board, being Jewish, I had fish cakes instead of bacon. On this particular day, instead of bacon our cook broke out smoked pork chops for a substitute. The aroma was devastating, and I thought to myself, "what the heck. Debbie, I think for a change I'll join you guys and have the pork chops and fried eggs. Just to be sociable you understand". Much banter by the crew "Zan, you'll be sorry for this". Prophetic words.

My next watch was noon 'til 16h00 so I had lots of time to get on with my daily routine. I washed my T-shirts and jeans, wrung out in salt water. Did ablutions on foredeck. Stripped down to birthday suit. No time for modesty. In humid weather, the lassies usually stripped to the waist without the restriction of bras. It was second nature and hardly a second glance given.

A heavy plastic bucket with a rope, knotted at intervals to get a strong purchase, and a crew member handy to help haul up the sea brine from the fast-moving waters was our shower. First wash all over with Elizabeth Ann baby shampoo and then slosh the seawater over your head and body and rinse the lot into the gunwales. This brand of shampoo the only one that would lather in sea water.

Then down into the cabin to clean the head, sweep the beautiful planked cabin floor and add a coat of liquid Cobra polish. Our bedding is always damp and musty smelling from the 90% humidity experienced at sea, so we put it outside on the pulpit with heavy pegs to clamp firm from the Force 3 breeze that's blowing. The cook on duty never does the dishes or pots and pans. Privilege of the cook. Although Sheralee and Debbie did a lot of the cooking, we all at one time of another helped out with our specialties. Mine was omelettes and fish cakes. A magic time for all of us was an hour, just before sunset. We would break out snacks and hors d'oeuvres, sometimes freshly smoked fish, right out of the ocean. Each of the crew with his or her favourite tipple. Usually Bells whisky, beer or cane and tonic, and we would watch the most unbelievable sunsets imaginable.

17th May 1983

01h00: The graveyard shift. Paul and Zan's first watch of the new day. We would be off by 05h00, after the usual four-hour stint. Then it was eight hours sleep and recreation. Reading, writing mail, listening to the interminable Joan Armatrading singing Drop the Pilot, ad nauseum at full decibels. Ear drum popping stuff. My Beethoven and Mozart tapes never touched the reproduction heads of the tape player.

Royco Instant Soup, on the hour, every hour, to ward off the cold and hunger pangs. One thing about going to sea in a small boat, the constant heaving and movement unconsciously caused one's muscular systems to create an equal and opposite reaction in a natural way, which culminated in unbelievable generating of the appetite. One was always hungry. Due to the lack of jogging space, ankles tended to swell up and retain water, creating stiffness. My yoga exercises on the poop deck, initially was grounds for much merriment, but in the long run paid dividends.

02h00: Barometric pressure 1013, windspeed 15 knots. Compass heading 300 degrees. Yacht surrounded by prancing dolphins, outpacing us. The waters fluorescent in the moonlight. Absolute magic. Our wake a rooster's tail of blended colours. Our bow slicing in to the ocean of salt water and churning up waves on to the playful dolphins. Mile after mile, having fun.

02h30: Barometric pressure 1012

15h00: Barometric pressure 1011 and falling, fast. Wind dying down.

15h30: Barometric pressure 1010. Becalmed. Absolutely flat sea. Clear skies. Sails flapping listlessly. Andy Jackson in his jockeys, makes an appearance up the gang ladder. Like a good skipper, in his sleep, knowing every movement of his boat, every change of course. Once on one of my watches, daydreaming at the helm, I went off course by 15 degrees and Andy was out of his bunk and upside wanting to know what the hell was going on when I made a sharp correction.

On this occasion he yelled "Hey guys, what's up?". "Skipper take a look at the barometer." "Oh, my Gawd," was his retort, "I'm going back to bed but when the Barometer bottoms out at 1000, give me call".

16h00: A half hour after Andy was on deck, we are on 1000 and Paul goes down the companionway to Skippers luxury quarters to give Andy the latest figure. Ten minutes later Andy is topside, all buttoned up in his orange heavy weather Sou'wester. The wind starts picking up. "Lads we are in for some nasty weather". Looking 100 kilometres dead ahead of us we can see mountainous, black storm clouds boiling on the surface of the water and building up to the ceiling of the heavens.

7 THE STORM

We are now in a trough of low pressure and the reading bottoms out at 900. "Zan", shouts Andy, "get below, I want all hands top side, on the double".

Graham and Debbie were difficult to wake. They had just completed their watch, with hardly two hours sleep under their belt. With much shaking, prodding and pulling the covers askew, I finally got them bleary-eyed but awake and compos mentis. Then to Gary and Sheralee. The same story. Much moaning and grumbling. "Is this absolutely necessary?" was the unspoken questions. Orders is orders, not to question, but to obey.

All the crew topside now, togged out in their foul weather oils. Instructions barked out by the boss, with a sense of urgency. All guys help to reef down the main sail and jib. The "coffee grinder" (two handed winch) working overtime and getting hot with the friction of the nylon ropes. Getting the job done in double quick time, sheets are coiled down on the deck and then the main sail covers on the boom securely strapped down. Hurricane winds seeping in to a loose edge could billow the whole thing into oblivion.

All the while now the rain started lashing down and the wind gusting in from all directions. Now's the time to start panicking. All hands buckle up our safety harnesses, clipped to the guard rails. A man overboard in this weather has no chance of recovering him on board. This was one of the many drills we practiced, in case someone or something valuable went overboard and needed retrieval. There was a very important formula, learnt by skippers for this eventuality. In our case, Andy would drop a small cork overboard. In a blow of eight knots he would take a timing at 30 seconds in the present heading. Then make a 90 degree turn to starboard for 40 seconds, then a further 90 degree turn to starboard for another 30 seconds. Lo and behold, we would be bearing down on the bobbing cork, like magic. In the case of a man going overboard, we would immediately toss after him a flag on an aluminium pole, mounted on a floatation sphere with which we could pinpoint his position. Hauling a man with his soaked clothing on board, in a gentle breeze of only five knots, took the strength of five able bodied seamen. Imagine the impossibility in a force ten blow.

Further preparations now. The jib sheet was hauled down. This is the sail attached to the bow of the boat on the baby stay. This is Gary's speciality. The baby boom for the spinnaker lashed down and the inflatable rubber duck firmly stowed on the aft deck. All the portholes and hatch cover tightly screwed down. All this is done while the seas are becoming very angry. Now we are no longer tacking in to the wind but have made a

180 degree about turn to run with the wind and the running seas.

Instead of heading due North to the Mediterranean, we are heading south. Back to where we had just come. We were, at this stage, 10 days out of Cape Town and the wind is picking up alarmingly.

Graham was rummaging around the sail bags looking for the storm sheet, stowed deep below decks in the forward locker. A most important item for survival in these conditions. This sail is only about 3 square metres in size and is utilized instead of, and in the same mounting position, as the jib. The hurricane force winds would billow this postage stamp sail in the direction of the following wind, keeping the bow of the boat from plunging into the raging surf and, at the same time, giving us a very respectable speed of knots.

These are not conditions for an inexperienced crew member to be at the helm. Andy and Graham would take the first watch and, two hours later, Gary would take over from Graham. There was no way Andy would come below under these conditions. Being the Skipper, and the most experienced of the crew, come hell or high water, he would have it no other way. Andy had many a tale to tell of his adventures in deep keel sailing. It was just recently he and a friend went to the aid of an American couple, in deep trouble off the East London coast. They could thank their lucky starts for their rescue by these intrepid South Africans.

At sea, one can actually see squalls, or storms approaching. It gives you some time to make preparations, in the first instance by reducing sail. Now we were well and truly in the vortex of the hurricane. Paul, myself, Debbie and Sheralee were below decks, firmly strapped in to our bunks. When I first got on board, I noticed these leather straps attached to the bunks, and wondered at the time what their purpose was. I realised later that they were there for rough weather. How bad could it get that we would actually need them?

Before getting horizontal we made sure that all glassware and crockery was firmly stowed in their holders. The cupboard doors tightly shut, and the gimballed gas stove wired down. The pots and pans secured under the galley wash basin.

Our movements in the cabin were restricted. In our hurry to haul down all the wet sails from upside, we literally dragged and bundled them down the gangway and stuffed them in to all nooks and crannies of the living area. On to the bunks, under the dining table, on top of the table, all the way up to the ceiling. By this time the vessel was tumbling in every direction of the compass, battered by a very angry and willful sea. Everything was in uncontrolled motion and, we were clinging on to every conceivable upright pillar or protuberance to prevent being dashed to the floor, or against immovable furniture. In addition, we all thought by this time we had acclimatized and were immune to the ravishes of seasickness. But, even

Sheralee and Andy, who were the only ones up to this time that had not been afflicted by this curse, would in the next few minutes, join the ranks of us mere mortals. We were reduced to being dizzy, nauseated and disorientated, and finally vomiting uncontrollable. With the boat tilting, for most of the time, at an angle of anything up to 75 degrees to 90 degrees from the port side, and then swinging violently in the opposite direction, the head (toilet) became completely useless. No matter how one pumped the flushing arm, no suction could be produced to drain the effluent. A veritable queue of pitiful individuals was lining up for relief. Little did we realise, at this time, that after the initial attempt to control our bodily function and use the facilities provided for this purpose, forty eight hours of ungovernable fury would confine us to straight jacket existence. The toilet was out of bounds.

What we experienced for those next two days is something I have thought of many a time in the years to follow. I came to the conclusion that it is an almost impossible task. Unless one has actually gone through this encounter with the convulsive, hissing, boiling, heaving, gyrating, whirling, colliding, explosive, volcanic forces manifested by the awesome powers of Mother Nature, it is hopeless to even attempt to describe it. Some of those adjectives may help to give you an idea.

A simple analogy would be to imagine yourself being popped in to an automatic washing machine, but worse. Not only would you be circulated in one direction, but in an instant, in the reverse direction. Then, in addition you would be thrown forward and backward, plunging into the raging surf and lurching and gyrating upwards toward the raging heavens, foul with black thunderclouds turning the darkness of night blacker than the depths of hell.

I am sure some of my readers will have done the crossing in an ocean liner from South African to the United Kingdom, and anticipated the fear instilled by those who have experienced it and told their harrowing accounts of the atrocious expanse of water known as the Bay of Biscay. I have had that experience at its worst behaviour. Believe me, in comparison to what we went through on Black Jed, the old Union Castle Liner's trip was an absolute picnic. A stroll through a tranquil meandering meadow fountain.

Luckily for most of us, we vomited topside when the violent buffeting turned our stomachs inside out and upside down. This relieved us to a certain extent, but the continual gagging when our innards had nothing further to contribute to the flotsam, left us weak and helpless. Confused in the mind, blinded by wind and driving salt spray and strangling our breathing we were deprived of all muscular power, bereft of all energy, weak in the knees and limp in the arms. Reflexes became as those of a newborn infant.

All this time, Andy was at the wildly gyrating helm, straining with all his might to anticipate where the next cascading tonnage of sea spray, foam and surf would converge. Suddenly, like a car slamming in to a brick wall, Black Jed would come to a complete standstill, as if gripped in the jaws of the devil, before having the living daylights shaken out of it.

From a flaccid ocean, when the barometer was at its ebb, the wind steadily built in strength, rising to a high screaming pitch of sound. In the background from far astern, came the sound of a herd of galloping buffalo. The gusting hurricane came roaring, screeching, wailing through the halyards, rigging, ropes, cables and rigmarole of the upper structures of the yacht.

The vast mass comprising hundreds of tons of water lurched violently against the hull, hitting the sides, bow and stern of our valiant little craft, producing a booming and banging of unbelievable intensity. This blended with the terrible din of the cataract of sound from the unleased fury of the tempest.

The wind was getting stronger and stronger. We could feel a new movement of the ocean. The swells were swinging to a raging rhythm. One instant we were peaking at the top of a crest, looking down to a valley forming 10 metres below us. It was like a nightmare when you dream of falling off a cliff. The little speck of our boat would surf down at an alarming rate to the bottom of the trough. On both sides of us were towering walls of water, blocking out the horizons. All you could see above was black cirrus clouds scudding under low lying evil cumulus nimbus, spouting forked tongues of lightening that snaked in to the heavens, lighting up the grotesque panorama playing out below. It was like a scene from Dante's Inferno.

I believe the famous composer, Johan Strauss Jnr., was an enthusiastic small yacht sailor. I think he got his inspiration from the Thunder and Lightning Polka when, one day he and a Viennese companion experienced a stormy day on the Danube. His composition is a true reflection of the agony of the violent devastation of the elements, and the ecstasy of eventual deliverance.

The needle on the windspeed meter now jammed firmly up against the maximum stop of 100 knots. We most probably were in the teeth of the hurricane, gusting at 135 knots. An ever present concern now was that our mast could be struck by lightning. Being made of aluminium it would be a perfect conductor. A more serious worry was that it could be snapped in half like a matchstick and swept overboard, taking all our rigging and stanchions, to which all our safety harnesses were attached. This is immediately followed by the anxiety that this event would take the crew overboard in to the raging waters.

Our lifeboat containing first aid kit, emergency flares, condensing unit for water, drag line for fishing, emergency food, torch, knives and more was on standby, lashed down midships. It is buckled down in such a fashion that it can be released in a jiffy. The ever possibility of us being swamped and submerged by the mass of water smashing down on us in a watery avalanche was not an unlikely scenario.

Down below decks, Paul and myself shared a small cabin. I was in the lower bunk. Debbie and Sheralee were in the main cabin. Graham and Gary alternated in keeping Andy company at the helm. We were all firmly strapped in to our bunks with the heavy duty leather belts, without which we would have been tossed about the cabin like limp rag dolls. Lying there prostrate, hour after hour, one's senses smashed to smithereens by the constant twisting, screwing motion, listening to the unbelievable thunderous, deafening booms of water breaking on our little craft, felt as if I had a rock band drummer incessantly banging his drum half an inch from my ear.

Constantly though my numbed mind, over and over, in snatches of semi consciousness, words of supplication ran. "The Lord is my shepherd; I shall not want. He leadeth me beside still waters". That's as far as I got. Over and over and over "He leadeth me beside the still waters; Still Waters, Still Waters". The most appropriate of prayers.

In my tortured dreams, my subconscious trying, without success, to block out the nightmare unfolding all around us, I remembered the day I left on my epic adventure. I went to say farewell to my old friend Jay Shifren. When I said goodbye, I mentioned as an afterthought, that I was doing a trip on a small yacht from Africa to Europe. His reaction was that of disbelief. "Zan, you must be mad. Don't go, I'll never see you again". In my demented state of mind, I now kept hearing Jays voice; "I'll never see you again", and I thought to myself, "Jay, you were right. This is the end of me".

Jays words were prophetic in that he passed away peacefully in his sleep on a quiet and tranquil night, safely in his bed. He never saw me again.

I never did have a normal sized bladder and it was usual for me to wake two or three times during the night. In this nightmare I was strapped in my bunk with my bladder at bursting point after five hours of hell. I was trying to hold it all together whilst putting off the inevitable. However, the time came, and I made the effort. Listlessly unstrapping myself, heaving myself out of my bunk whilst weak in the arms and legs and nauseous, holding on to the uprights, table legs, book racks and steering myself to the heads with misplaced optimism of actually accomplishing an impossible task. Our little yacht was pitching and rolling uncontrollably to all points of the compass as I tried to wade through, over and under acres of sails, hurriedly stowed and choking up the companionway and cabin. Eventually, slouched over the toilet pan, swaying all over the place and hanging on to the overhead plumbing, I tried to relax and allow gravity to take over and relieve myself naturally. Looking down at the stench and solids slopping all over the place it was a near impossibility.

Nothing now but to fight my way back to my bunk. Then calamity struck. A particularly vicious lurch of the boat swung me around, my left shoulder smashing into the bulkhead with all the force of a sledgehammer. In stunned dismay I realised that my left arm had dislocated. Over the years this has been a recurrent problem for me. In anguish I called out, "Heaven help me". Being a believer, I am firmly convinced of the power of divine intervention. Losing my grip my body swaying all over the place, another vicious lurch of the boat swung me around again in the opposite direction. My left shoulder once more taking the brunt of an impact against another immovable locker. Lo and behold! My left arm slotted right back into the socket. Against all laws of medical physiotherapy.

I literally crawled back to my bunk, now so weak and nauseated my head aching fit to burst and losing the will to live. "Oh my God! Please let me die; enough is enough".

Exhausted, I drifted off in to a deep, deep sleep, while all around me the living hell continued. The most vivid dreams of high intrigue and adventure helped blot out the reality in the merciless, ferocious world around me.

8 SILENCE

The silence was deafening. All around me, serenity. I awoke and with my eyes still closed I thought to myself, this is unreal. Am I in heaven? The boat was completely still. Absolutely no motion and gentle water lapping against the hull.

I opened my eyes and peered through the cabin door. Inert bodies lying prone and still with the sound of heavy snoring. Music to my ears. I, together with my crew mates had survived. I just could not believe that we had emerged from a living nightmare. Andy was the real hero. His tenacity, experience, physical and mental stamina in outwitting Neptune and natures forces and escaped the invitation to a watery grave on the sea bed below was an inspiration to us all.

The next day prominently displayed on the bulletin board was a new notice.

Now for the big clea n up and dry out. The first job

> **Notice to Catering Staff.**
> *From this day forward, until further notice, any crew member guilty of serving bacon, pork, ham or any non-kosher food to Zan Swartzberg, shall be guilty of a serious offence and will be subject to the following punishment.*
> *Walk the plank, keelhauling and confinement to Bosun's locker room for 1000 days, without compassion or reduction in sentence for good behavior.*
> *If said Zan Swartzberg is caught in the act of such transgression, he shall summarily be dissected for shark bait.*
> **Signed by order of the Captain: Andrew Jackson (Judge and Jury).**

was to get all the sodden sails topside and draped over the decks to dry out before hoisting the essential ones. The others, such as the spinnakers were neatly folded with rubber bands in the correct strategic positions and stowed in their bags. When they are hoisted the rubber bands snap in the wind, making it easier to position in a strong blow.

The beautiful velvet cushions down below were completely soaked, and a strong smell of sea salt permeated the entire cabin. These were hung up on the rigging and after a few days, dried out. Unfortunately, their colour and shape did not quite return to the original. Half a metre of water in the bilges had to be removed. Buckets and pumps worked overtime with many willing hands taking turns when weakened muscles gave out. It felt like our arms and legs had been stuffed with cotton wool after the two days of enforced fasting. The charts, maps, pilot books and library books were all water logged, some beyond redemption.

Most of the fresh provisions, such as onions, oranges, bread and other veggies were completely ruined and were reluctantly thrown overboard, with much regret. Next inspection was the bunk lockers, into which a ton of canned foods had been stowed. Baked beans, sweetcorn, pickles, asparagus, mixed veggies, jams, canned fruit, canned fish, bottled sauces etc. By the time we did our inspection all the labels had come off and, within a few days, the tins started rusting. This did not matter too much but, when it came to the opening of a tin, it was a little like Russian Roulette. What you thought was beans turned out to be shrimps in brine, or peaches. All the packaged goods were completely ruined. Biscuits, custard powder and our magnificent selection of sweets, crisps and nuts were gone. Enough to drive one to melancholia.

On the first evening after the storm, looking southwestward, we could clearly see in the distance, reflected against a black bank of cloud, the lights of Cape Town. They were winking and blinking at us, beckoning us to come back home.

The subject was never discussed, but I am sure we were all, in the back of our minds, cogitating on packing up and abandoning the project.

A sign of weakness?

We were made of sterner stuff than that!

9 LET'S TRY AGAIN

Logbook notes
22nd May 1983.
Let's try again.

It is now two days after our terrible ordeal. We have new meaning to our lives. What we went through as a team and survived has induced an exquisite tolerance to each other's petty foibles, which previously would spark irritation and unconscious ill feeling. I was actually quite willing to accept Joan Armatrading belting out "Drop the Pilot" until the cows came home. I was a privilege just to be alive and I was happy to now say au revoir to Mozart and Beethoven.

10h30: Barometer 1016. So why is the weather so boisterous? Trade winds are blowing fresh at a steady 15 to 20 knots. Whistling Jack was present in the form of a steady high-pitched whistle, which was very reassuring. A sure sign that we are making good headway, gusting along at a true speed of about 8 knots. According to our last "fix", we are now approximately 1800 kilometres from St Helena. If we keep this speed over a 24 hour day we will log 360 kilometres a day and should catch sight of our landfall in about five days. Weather permitting and God willing.

Our self-steering apparatus is working perfectly now. By some obscure attachment to the rudder, sails and steering mechanism, one sets the course according to the compass heading and lo and behold, the boat steers itself. Like magic! So, we named it Merlin. It's just like having automatic pilot on an aircraft. Hand's free for miles of limitless ocean. You can make yourself comfortable behind the wheel, which is perpetually in motion adjusting to the various small changes of wind speed and direction.

When we first arrived on board this devious device just would not co-operate. Andy, with the persistence of Job, and the help of Gary and Graham, finally got the better of the intricacies of this most wonderful gadget. Worth its weight in Scotch mist. We had been hand steering up until now, with the continual physical strain of hands on the wheel, watching the compass and horizon to make adjustments to course and keeping a watch for obstructions and shipping ahead, especially at night. After a four hour watch it was mind bending.

Normally from Cape Town, with fair trade winds, the journey to St Helena takes 12 days for a distance of 2700 kilometres almost due north. The Island is about 122 square kilometres.

Coming in to St Helena and seeing the Island towering out of the sea in a cloud of mist, was the most wonderful feeling of wellbeing. Especially for our skipper, Andy Jackson. This was his first Trans-Atlantic experience and he was not quite sure of his navigational skills with the sextant. This ancient piece of equipment was used by all the great explorers of the past, including the likes of Vasco Da Gama, Nelson and Columbus. The principle remained the same. An accurate time schedule (thank heavens for the BBC pips), an accurate chart of the night skies, and the sun and moon (when the weather was good). It has mostly been replaced now by modern, scientific methods such as Satellite navigation which allows you to press a button and your position is available.

For us, we took our sights using the old-fashioned method of the Sextant. When we saw a merchant or fishing ship, we would take our sight, call up the vessel and ask them for a navigational fix. At sea, a brotherhood of great camaraderie exists, unlike anything else in the world. After a nice chat on the radio telephone, they would produce their figures. Invariably Andy's figures were spot on. In rough weather though a sextant fix was extremely difficult as the equipment requires to be held rock steady. Always a chance the skipper and sextant could go overboard while take a sight in rough weather.

Too bad about the skipper; we could always get along without him at a pinch, but with the sextant gone we could end up in the Antarctic!

At least by the time you got to Antarctic it would be too late to know you were not supposed to be there. The freezing conditions could eliminate you along with the lack of supplies.

25th May 1983

It is now 17 days since we left Cape Town and we were all ready to get ashore for a hot shower or bath. It wasn't that easy when we arrived a St Helena. There was no quayside like normal harbours where you could just drop your sails and, in a controlled way, motor in to a berth and tie up like civilized sailors, step ashore, wobble around for a while in a dizzy spell before getting your land legs. A very strange feeling stepping on to land after being at sea for so long. The earth moves around and unbalances your movements.

About a kilometre from the shoreline we dropped anchor. It was at a depth of about 30 metres before our anchor chain lost its slack. Then came the innumerable but essential routine jobs that needed to be done before we could go ashore.

Haul down the main sail, stow it under canvas. Haul down the jib and spinnaker and pack them into their respective bags which then had to be stowed in their lockers. They needed to be folded up in the correct manner to avoid entanglements and problems when hoisting them later. By now, after doing this so many times since leaving East London, it came naturally to us, under the ever watchful eyes of our very, very strict skipper. East London, Port Elizabeth, Mossel Bay, Cape Town; the same ritual over and over again. It had to be exactly right and no half measures.

The biggest job of all was to take the dinghy out of mothballs. In all our other ports of call we had a berth and did not need our own ship to shore transport. St Helena and Ascension Island are both British protectorates. It seems the British were not interested in upgrading these two islands under their control. No profit in that!

We finally managed to wrestle the waterproofed bundle containing all the bits and pieces of the dinghy out of its holding harness and, with much kibitzing from the rabble, Graham and Gary finally got the framework assembled, the pontoons blown up and the small 3hp Suzuki outboard engine mounted to the transom. It had not been used for months and, with the help of some blasphemous language, we got the Suzuki fired up.

After all the hatches and port holes had been meticulously battened down to prevent any exposure to the elements, and a small miserable lock for the hasp and staple on the main entry (not much help if intruders paid a visit) all eight crew crammed, thigh to thigh, in the narrow confines of our little dinghy. Andy at the helm, the Suzuki spluttered away contentedly, and the salt spray whipped over the bow in to our faces as we headed for civilization. Brilliant!

There were about ten other yachts anchored in the roadway (as the bay is called). Detouring close to them we saw some familiar faces from Cape Town. Excited waving on both sides, but no time to stop and get the latest gossip. Where to water our horses, snack emporiums not to be missed and pitfalls to avoid is all essential information one picks up, as naturally as breathing, in the yachting scene.

10 TIME ASHORE

The main town in St Helena, beside many small villages, is Jamestown with a population of about 5000 souls. The language is English, spoken with a distinctive accent by the far-flung British subjects that had come to live here.

The two distinctive aspects of life on the island. The first is that there is absolutely no crime. Whilst we were there for the first time in living memory, a murder was committed. The suspect was the only tenant in the local jail and was due to be repatriated for trial in England as there were no facilities available for a conviction of this nature on the Island.

The other wonderful thing, especially for the bachelors on the Island, is that males were outnumbered by three to one by females. What a paradise! It made no difference if you were a local man or a visiting yachtsman, the place to congregate was the local Disco. The usual programme would be a social function at the local church hall for tea and cookies, table tennis, tenniquoits, bingo and handball until 10pm. Then the Fathers would shut up shop. Then the disco would continue until the early hours of the morning, with the usual combination of alcoholic lubrication, the deafening roar of the latest rock and roll and disco music and the welcome invitation of the lasses. It all made for a wonderful, relaxing evening.

After this we had the hazardous boarding of the yacht. In our inebriated state, we try to get into the dinghy without first getting dunked in to the ice cold waters of the Atlantic. It would have been an instant cure for sozzled souls.

Back in the early 1800's, St Helena was one of the main islands for the hunting of whales. It was the mainstay of the economy. Strangely, the usual type of fishing was non-existent. Unlike further south the warm Benguela current off the coast of South West Africa didn't reach St Helena. When the whaling industry petered out, the British encouraged the St Helenian farmers to plant a crop of Flax. From flax they could produce string. All the string was sold to the British Post Office, a ready-made market until polypropylene was discovered. It was far stronger and a fraction of the price of the St Helena string.

The industrious St Helena women are world famous for the beautiful lace work. The craft is handed down over centuries from mother to daughter. When the flax and hemp production shut down, many jobs were lost by the menfolk. Many of them got a free ride to the Island of Ascension, about 1200 kilometres north. A small 5000 ton tanker owned by the Admiralty made the trip once a month to bring supplies of petrol to the islanders. These men were given jobs working on Ascension for the British, who maintained a very important Royal Air Force Base, a cable communication network and the usual harbour facilities. The Americans were also there with a Satellite tracking station. This was the reason for the dire lack of male company for the females on St. Helena.

On our daily trips to shore from the yacht, we would pass close to the tanker which was anchored close to our mooring. With a friendly wave to their crew we eventually met their skipper. He had at his disposal the company Ford Transit Mini Bus. On his invitation he took us, and the crew of a Mauritian yacht, for a drive all over the island. There was no such thing as a tourist bus, so he acted as our guide, telling us all about the Island.

One of the interesting farms we visited was high up in the mountains where the rainfall was a hefty 1000mm a year (10mm at sea level). They grew abundant vegetables, had herds of dairy and beef cows and a large piggery. All of which were used to feed the inhabitants and revictual the many yachts and passing tourist and merchant shipping.

The Island had a large British contingent of civil servants, headed by the Governor on the island. It is the administrative centre for all the Islands under British control; Ascension, Tristan da Cunha, Gough and two islands with the unlikely names of Nightingale and Inaccessible

We noticed a lot of layabouts sitting around contentedly, sipping coffee at the side walk cafes, or loitering around the myriad of bars in abundance. At the main entrance to the Governor's Office on the notice board is a sign giving the scheduled times for when the 'dole' was paid out, when free milk powder was available, when the dental unit would be there and when the free medical team would be in attendance. All at the cost of the British tax payer.

Except for the icy cold waters of the South Atlantic, the weather was amazingly mild and agreeable, with a south easterly trade wind blowing most of the year. There was no smog or smoke to damage the respiratory system. These trade winds were what all yachtsman timed their journeys for heading north to Europe and America or the British Isles. One had a narrow margin of error and, if you got your timing wrong, you could land up on the equator in the doldrums.

We found an eatery called Anne's Café. It was known far and wide in the yachting fraternity, for their marvelous fish and pork dishes and the local delicacies, at tariffs to make a gourmet's mouth water. Every evening, all the yotties in the harbour would gather at Anne's, where tables were set out in a beautiful garden under awning made of thatch grass. This is what we call living. The camaraderie and fellowship under those conditions, knowing the expertise and dangers your fellow yotties experienced, formed a bond of unbelievable depth. From Anne's we would invariably get together on one of the other yachts for a night cap. Inevitably ending in the early hours, after lots of conversation, singing and smoking. We seldom slept in our own bunks whilst in port.

Yacht crews, like tourists all over the world, were keen and eager to take in all the usual places of interest. A must on our list was to visit the place where Napoleon Bonaparte spent his last five year of his life. Banished to St Helena where he could get up to no more mischief after losing the Battle of Waterloo, he was buried on St. Helena but was allowed to be re-interred in France many years later.

After a two hour hike north of Jamestown, through beautiful small holdings, we finally arrived at the magnificent "Longwood" house, where Napoleon and his entourage lived in comparative luxury. This is where he wrote his memoirs during the years 1815 to 1821.

After the British East Indian Company annexed the Island from the Portuguese, a garrison of English soldiers were stationed there in 1673 to protect the inhabitants. These engineers found a natural reservoir of water on top of one of the volcanic outcrops close to the harbour. To get to the top they constructed a pathway of very steep steps, with guard rails on each side to cling to while ascending. The notice at the bottom of the steps warns that you climb at your own risk. 999 steps to the top! We recommend that you take the advice of those with knowledge. On your way up – Don't Look Down!

At the top, one gets a magnificent view of the harbour, James Bay .and the town. Fortunately, there is an alternative round down, via a road winding down the side of the mountain.

Whilst wandering through the back alleys of the village, we stumbled across a very little publicized monument erected to Joshua Slocum. He was an American, and the first yachtsman to ever sail around the world single handed, back in the 1800's. It was quite an achievement. Those old timber constructed sloops with old fashioned hemp ropes, canvas sails which would become heavily waterlogged in the lightest mist or drizzle, made the manhandling of equipment in heavy seas extremely difficult.

Joshua Slocum, whilst rounding Cape Horn in the Southern Ocean, on his way to the Cape of Good Hope, presumably got caught in the giant seas generated by terrible hurricanes, and notoriously known as the Roaring Forties. He was never heard of again. Those were the days when radio communication was an unknown luxury. His friends and family could only speculate as to when and where he lost his life. Truly a most amazing giant in the era of single handed, small boat sailing.

One of the many characters we met on the Island was a German expatriate, by the name of Werner Schultz. Werner owned a rusty old steel hulled boat. Not a yacht and not a tramp steamer, but something in between. With a mast for a set of sails and a 30kw inboard diesel engine to motor him out of the doldrums on his many trips from St. Helena to Rio de Janeiro in the Argentines. One of the laws on St. Helena is that only St. Helenians could obtain trading licences. Werner had a girlfriend from the Island who had a small licensed shop selling a variety of goods ranging from canned foods to haberdashery and clothing. It all depended on Werner. Whenever stocks ran low, he would single handedly traipse off to Argentina, or one of the other South American countries and fill up his holds with whatever stock for the shop that took his fancy. He also indulged in horse trading, exchanging some of the local products such as lace. He made a good living, and he deserved every penny he made. The arduous 4000 kilometre trip could take up to two months. But he loved the life and anything to do with the sea, from sailing to scuba diving and fishing.

After 7 days on the Island, Andy decided we had rested long enough and before we lost the benefit of the trade winds, we had better make a move. Andy was the sales manager for the Mercedes Benz factory in East London and had only 3 months leave so he had a strict time table to adhere to.

On our last evening with Werner, he promised to give us a sendoff when we left the next morning at sun rise. After the attendant preliminaries to our next leg, up to Ascension, and with our jerry cans topped up with diesel, water kegs replenished, fresh fruit and vegetables stowed, our universal currency of bartering Bell's Whiskey and Werner as our middle man, we lacked for nothing at the most unbelievable advantageous prices.

11 BEST LAID PLANS

2nd June 1983

We all thought it was now plain sailing. Gary went forward to switch on the electric winch to haul up the anchor. The chain started winding on to the winch drum, pulling Black Jed forward, whilst the slack was taken up.

Then, to our astonishment, the bow of the yacht started dipping slowly and inexorable down into the ocean. Before Gary could react and switch off the winch, our bow dipped below the surface of the ocean. Andy yelled out instructions to Gary to cut the power, but it was too late. We had visions of the whole caboodle sinking into oblivion. Fortunately salt water and electrics do not mix. As the winch got swamped the water shorted out the motor with much steam and hissing sounds. We all sighed a collective prayer of thanks to the old man of the sea, Father Neptune.

It was obvious that our anchor had snared some obstacle on the sea bed. Werner, who was standing by in his dinghy alongside of us, donned his snorkel and flippers and, in the twinkling of an eye, was overboard to investigate the problem. A few minutes later he surfaced to give us the bad news that our anchor had snagged on an old engine block. These blocks were scattered on the sea floor and were used with chains and floats in the old days when fishing boats made berth.

We could have hacksawed the anchor chain to release us from bondage, but that meant losing our anchor, an essential item for mooring. At any rate Taffy, the owner, would definitely not be charmed at the prospect of having to buy a replacement.

Werner kindly offered to go ashore and collect one of his mates with underwater acetylene equipment to cut the tip of our anchor points. By the time a suitably attired expert, in his diving suit and steel helmet, with oxygen tanks and cutting equipment finally arrived and cut us free, it was well after midday. This time is wasn't Bells Whiskey but 200 US Dollars that did the trick. With our electric winch out of action, it was now elbow grease to winch up the anchor, together with the weight of the attached 500 kg chain.

As we headed north to Ascension it was well after midday. The Island was named by the Portuguese explorer and navigator Da Nova, who landed there in the year 1501 on Ascension Day. Hence the name.

As we left the anchorage, we set the course with compass reading 235 degrees. Barometric pressure 1016, temperature 20 degrees Celsius.

Latitude 13°56' S, 8° 35' W. Approximately 1100 kilometres to Ascension. Number One sheet down and the Tri Radial Spinnaker up. Running our donkey (our pet name for the diesel engine) for two hours to charge batters, running the lights, freezer and radio equipment. We have lots of perishables, such as meat, fish, ice cream and ice cubes in the freezer.

We trolled for, and caught, two Bonitos. By the time we got them on board half their bodies had been ripped to pieces by following sharks. Nevertheless, we gutted what was left of them. In to the stainless steel smoker with Finnish sawdust and on to the gimballed gas stove. Within an hour the most delicious and tender smoked fish was ready for eating.

Heading 110 to 120 degrees South East.

It took us five days to reach Ascension. The pattern of our days was repetitive. A steady South East Trade Wind pushed us along at a steady 8 knots. No shortage of fresh fish. In the mornings we invariably caught small flying fish in the sails. They were very tasty. We also caught Bonito regularly with our trolling line and a very bright aluminium lure attached to our transom.

6th June 1983
08h00: Barometric pressure 1014 to 1016. Sighted Ascension Island.
12h00: Berthed alongside the quay.

Our first impression was most depressing. Petrol and oil storage tanks, warehouses, workshops and gantries for unloading cargo on to tenders.

The Island is the result of a volcanic upheaval over one million years ago. It is about 90 square kilometres of volcanic rock and was established by the British. Georgetown made up of 1500 residents is mostly young men who found work with the Americans, British telecoms, Port authority, BBC and Royal Air Force.

Babies born on the Island, although British subjects, were registered as being born at sea and the location of the birth being an obscure village somewhere in England.

An impressive jumble of rocks rising to a height of 1000 metres above sea level was known as Green Mountain. It had a catchment area for rain water and beyond in a valley was a forest of Pine and Fir trees established by sea farers of old. They used the Island as a half way station to the Far East before the days of the Suez Canal. The trees were standing about 30 metres and were straight and tall. The old sea farers would land in Ascension and, if they had been dismasted, they would simply cut a tree to use as a replacement mast.

Exploring the many little bays and beaches on the Island, we came across a small graveyard. It was reserved strictly for those unfortunate soldiers who had died of yellow fever, an incurable disease in days past, and very contagious. It was sad to see the simple gravestones with the names and ages of the young men who died thousands of miles away from home, in the service of their country.

Also, on the Island was an airport with a runway suitable for taking the largest military and civilian aircraft. British Overseas Airway Corporation (BOAC) had a weekly charter to and from Britain. The thought constantly crossed my mind, night and day, whether I should opt out and book a flight directly to England. I continually berated and lectured myself. "Come on Swartzberg, don't take the easy way out. Pull yourself together. Think of the satisfaction in doing the full stretch". My better judgement prevailed.

The morning after arriving, our crew took a stroll through the town. On the outskirts we came across a sports field, boasting a cricket pitch and a small grandstand for spectators. A match was in progress and, for the novelty of it, we sat down next to a group of young men decked out in their cricket togs, waiting to take their turn at the crease.

Our two attractive crew members, Debbie and Sheralee, within seconds had attracted their attention and they were not slow in coming forward. After all, one did not have such luck in a month of Sundays. It was in the twinkling of an eye that they knew all about us and we knew all about them. They were Royal Air Force crew stationed on the base. Within no time at all we were made honourary members of their mess and invited to have supper with them that evening.

The next few days was most pleasantly spent being invited out to all their functions and sporting activities. The fuss they made over our two lassies was unbelievable but understandable, after all, they were the only two eligible females on the whole of the Island. Everything was on the house and we met a really nice bunch of guys. Highly qualified, professional fliers with no pretensions as to wealth and social aspirations.

I had the honour of being invited to play a round of golf with three of the guys. Why call it an honour? Well, according to the Guinness Book of Records, the gold course on the Island of Ascension, was considered to the "Worst Golf Course in the World". Eighteen holes built on rock larva. The greens comprised of fine gravelly stones. It had quite a respectable little club house. When one hit a shot with a driver and the ball bounced" just right" on the rocky fairway, it would travel in the vicinity of 500 metres, about twice the distance of a normal drive on a grass fairway.

Eventually it was time to leave on the next leg northwards. This was now to be the longest haul. Next stop the Portuguese Islands of the Azores.

Before leaving we replenished our stock of beer from the pub on the R.A.F base. Genuine Heineken beer, costing us the princely sum of 5 new

English pence per can!

The RAF command promised to give us a sendoff the next morning and, true to their word, a few hours after we left Ascension a huge four engine Hercules transport plane buzzed us, dangerously low. What a send off.

We worked out that it probably cost the British tax payer at least £17000 sterling for that dangerous exercise.

12 AZORES

9th June 1983

This is the longest leg of our trek. Up to the equator about 1200 kilometres away. Then on to the Portuguese islands of the Azores. Another 6500 kilometres. Should the winds be variable and requiring lots of tacking we could be sailing closer to 10000 kilometres. That would take us close to 30 days of hard sailing. We will have to be very judicious with our fresh water supply. On Andy's instructions fresh water for drinking and cooking purposes only. No more rinsing crockery, pots and pans or even brushing our teeth in fresh water.

19h00: Barometer 1012. Trade winds 15 to 20 knots south easterly. Compass heading 350 degrees. A strange sea. Flat as a pancake which is unusual with such a brisk breeze blowing. Spinnaker up.

It is very, very hot and humid. The Skipper instructs us to rig the awning amidships to give protection from the blazing sun. Great for us fair skinned types.

10th June 1983

A not so typical day. Heading 320 degrees. Trade winds co-operating like mad. Whistling Jack now at a high pitch. After 24 hours of non-stop billowing, we can see lots of wear and tear on the seams of the sail. We can clearly see ribbons of torn sail fluttering from the triangular corners of our beautiful multi-coloured patchwork Spinnaker. Then suddenly, like a crack of thunder, our spinnaker bursts at all the seams and ribbons of nylon cloth twitches every which way in the wind.

Black Jed, with surprising suddenness came to a standstill, wallowing around like a beached whale. Crew in various stages of off-duty activity; sleeping, reading, laundering, toiletries, playing chess and patience, like professionals, did not wait to be summoned and were topside in a flash. Each one knowing his duties to a tee. What a difference to the motley, inexperienced bunch we were not so many moons ago. I must take my hat off to Sheralee and Debbie. No quarter asked for or given. Two of the best "men" on the boat. In a heaving sea balancing on the bow is tough and dangerous work.

11th June 1983

Previous day log shows 245 kilometres. By Andy's reckoning we have another 400 before we reach the magical equator. Just before the end of my shift, a combination of weather conditions, temperature in the high 20 degrees Celsius and 90% humidity created a swirling white mist.

Ploughing through this into the breaking dawn, with sun rays creating a rainbow and reflecting beautiful red patterns on our sail, changing hues as the sun got higher and stronger, I recalled the song, Red Sails in the Sunset. Perhaps the composer was a yachtsman.

12th June 1983

10h00: Andy takes a sighting and decides that we are on the equator. Public Holiday for us all. Nobody mentions time during the journey and the days blend in to each other. Sundays are like any other day. We drop the sails. The seas are calm and in turn, we all go skinny dipping. Before going overboard, we apply lashings of Elizabeth Anne's baby shampoo all over. Gary in the bosun's chair is half way up the mast keeping a sharp look-out for tell take signs of sharks cruising and sniffing around for a change of diet. I have a nagging feeling of insecurity. First time equator crossers are summarily trussed up, shaving cream lavishly applied and unmercifully ragged and shaved with the blunt side of a carving knife.

2nd July 1983

It is the day before we make landfall at the port of Horta on the Island of Faial, the largest of the nine Portuguese islands of the Azores.

01h00: Dead calm, not a breath of wind. The sails are flapping listlessly. Paul Dugmore is on watch with me. The night is as black as the ace of spades. Eerie. The green and red navigational lights high up on the mast are casting a supernatural aura over our little kingdom. We are a speck of frail humanity in God's vast domain.

We dropped all the sails and fired up the donkey. Motored for four hours. As diesel was funning low we keep the revs down. Andy's instructions to save on fuel. Drinking water is also on rations. We have now been on the high seas for 23 days since leaving Ascension.

05h00: A zephyr of the lightest of breezes lifts our pennant. Pray like crazy that it strengthens. Hallelujah, it builds up to 2, then 3, then 4 knots and before long it's up to 8 knots. Hoisted the main sheet and jib. It billows out with the following wind. No need for tacking. Lovely smooth sailing, going along with the sea horses.

07h00: Horta visible with the binoculars, through the mist. We dropped and stowed all the sails with many willing hands. Mooring into Horta we see a great many yachts in the harbour. It's very popular with the sailors from all over the world. No berth available against the quay. We hoist the South African and Portuguese flags before docking.

As we are idling slowly along the concrete bluff looking for somewhere to moor, a foghorn of a voice hails us. "Dag julle ouens. Kom parkeer langs ons." (Good day you guys come park alongside us). We gladly accepted the invitation. Our benefactor, a tall Afrikaner dressed in khaki shirt and khaki trousers, with veldskoens and a floppy khaki hat. He looked like a typical Free State farmer, just off his tractor and settling down on the front stoep to drink his morning coffee.

His ketch is called Dolos (ketch is a two masted yacht). As kids we used to play with Dolos. They are yellow clay toys in the shape of oxen and made by the Sotho people.

Merriweather was a civil engineer who, whilst working for the East London Port Authority, invented a four pronged concrete device. The prongs are about 2 metres long and point in four different directions. The total weight of the contraption is about a ton. These devices are scattered one on top of the other on the sea bed. The prongs interlock and form an immovable mass. They are used to stabilize shifting sands due to currents caused by prevailing winds. They are now used all over the world, being cheap and very effective. They are called Dolos and, with a bit of imagination, you could visualize them looking a bit like the clay oxen.

In our travels we met many fascinating personalities, but this crew and boat were one for the books. The ketch was a homebuilt ferrocement construction. Similar to that of yacht Kya Lami that sank in East London at the start of our adventures.

I have been messing around boats all my life and had never come across an ugly boat until I met up with Dolos. The hull, a dull grey colour of natural cement, was streaked with rust trails where the water had penetrated the concrete skin, oxidizing the steel inner reinforcing. No attempt to titivate her cosmetically had been made by the owners.

She was a big 'un. At least 60 feet long and 20 feet broad in the mid section. No such niceties as portholes, upper ventilation channels or spray dodgers to protect the helmsman in rough and windy conditions. The cherry on the top was, and you won't believe this, the two masts. Something to be seen to be believed. Way back in the early part of the century, South Africa imported from England heavy, cast iron telephone poles, weighing a mass of kilograms. Two of these had been bought at a scrap yard and stepped, deep in the bowels, of Dolos. They seemed to serve two purposes. As part of the deep keel, lending stability and, of course, as an unyielding, unbreakable medium to hoist the main sails.

The crew were two brothers and their lone passenger, their invalid mother. Her mode of dress was typical of the Boer Vrou, billowing skirts and a traditional kappie. We often caught a glimpse of her, happily trundling herself around the deck in her wheelchair. She must have been well into her eighties. There they were, this unlikely trio, sailing the high seas. Not a care in the world and no pressures of keeping to an unforgiving timetable. I really admired these two caring yachtsmen who took pleasure in having an incapacitated, widowed mother with them, in the very inhospitable environs of an ocean going vessel. All well in calm seas, but imagine strapping her down, feeding and attending to her needs in stormy waters.

We had just completed the longest leg of our journey. Over 6000 kilometres from Ascension Island in 23 days. From the south Atlantic, through the equator and into the North Atlantic. The two main towns in the Azores are Horta on the Island of Faial and Ponta Delgado on Sao Miguel about 50 kilometres northwest. There was a very important British Naval Base there used during the last world war by the Allies for rest and recuperation as well as revictualling for the battleship and submarine convoys. The Portuguese, like their brethren across the world, are famous for their green fingers. The main crops on the Islands were prolific in vegetable, fruit and sugar beet production, as well as dairy and beef herds which thrived.

The Islands were discovered in 1432 by Vasco da Gama and were also visited by Columbus. They were formed by volcanic eruptions. The nine islands cover an area of around 890 square miles with a total population of 26,000 people.

The harbour and yacht basins were beautifully protected from the prevailing winds by a tall retaining wall. 5 metres high and 2 kilometres in length. All the visiting yacht crews inscribed on this wall their names and dates of their visit to Horta. Thousands and thousands of names were painted in all colours of the rainbow. Some in distinctive styles and some in a very artful way, making fascinating reading to all visitors to the port.

In the four days we spent in Horta, the only meal we had on board was breakfast. Lunches and suppers were eaten out, in the town which had many small restaurants serving the typical Portuguese fair. For the equivalent of 2 American dollars (about 85 south African cents) we could have a slap up meal. Hors d'oeuvres, fish course, meat course, vegetables and salad, desert, bread rolls with real butter and a bottle of wine.

We met many interesting people in Horta. One crew was an American, with his wife and baby daughter of around 2 years old. She happily toddled all over their yacht, most of the time without attention from her parents. She seemed to be instinctively aware of the dangers of failing overboard. He was an ex-Vietnam helicopter pilot and was on his way to Kuwait in the Middle East, where he was contracted to fly helicopters in the oil fields. His wife loved making pastry delicacies and spoiled our crew outrageously with these sweets. During the course of our friendship we learned that one of their crew members had just opted out of completing the journey, so Paul Dugmore from our crew offered to fill in and crew with them. They accepted his offer and so, Paul changed ships and finally ended up in Kuwait.

Another very interesting personality that we met on Horta was a middle-aged British yachtsman. He was sailing single handedly on a 20foot sloop from England to Brazil and back, on a fund-raising mission for children suffering with the incurable disease Spina Bifida. What was so unusual was that he was a paraplegic himself, completely paralysed from his chest down. We visited him on board and, solicitously offered to be helpful. He refused all physical aid. It was heartbreaking, but inspirational, to see him manoeuvre his lifeless body, in a specially fitted out wheelchair, around the strict confines of his small boat. An inspiration to us able-bodied types, moaning and groaning at the most trivial of discomforts.

3rd July 1983

Our second day in Horta. After breakfast the crew all went to the main harbour. The ablution blocks are well kept, clean and hygienic. All crews are welcome to use them for free. There was a short wait, but it wasn't long before the steam from piping hot water was washing away the grime and opening up the clogged pores. Most refreshing.

About two hours later we visited the shopping area, gift shops and post office, where we literally posted hundreds to cards to friends and relatives and were on our way home when Andy suddenly realised that he had forgotten his wristwatch on the washbasin of the ablution block. Fearing the worst, we hastily retraced our steps to this public amenity and, lo and behold, the watch was in the same place that he had left it. A very pleasant outcome and a demonstration of the honesty of the local peoples.

From there, strolling back on the way road to Black Jed's berth a pesky little black hound came rushing at us, barking and snapping at our heels. Andy let out a "Voetsak Brak!" and, with a loud yelp of anguish, the dog ran off with his tail between his legs We wondered if he was a pet on Dolos, or that the words uttered by Andy are one of those universal utterances understood by canines the world over.

6th July, 183

Time is running out for Andy, so we depart the safe haven of Horta. Next

stop is Porto del Gardo and San Miguel. Course 10 degrees South West. On motoring out to sea, at the end of the jetty, waving like a dervish is a one man farewell party. Paul Dugmore; taking pictures like crazy. I'm going to miss him and his tales of his previous adventures. His annual three monthly sojourns working on a kibbutz on Lake Tiberius in Israel, hoisting back breaking bunches of bananas to the curing sheds for export to Europe. His time of fishing boats in Newfoundland, in the bitter cold, netting 100 kilogram Sturgeon. The source of expensive caviar for the world's gourmets.

13 THE END OF THE LINE

9th July 1983

At last, our final leg to Portugal. Course 110 degrees. Wind 15 knots. Approximate distance to travel 2000 kilometres.

10th July 1983

Absolutely not a breath of wind. We are becalmed. All the sails are down. The diesel engine is driving us along at a steady pace of 5 knots an hour with a steady drone, hour after hour of monotonous throbbing and vibration. We siphon diesel from our plastic drums in to the main tank, refueling our engine. We are experiencing the doldrums. At least we can motor out of it. In the old days of sailing ships, they could get mired in this for weeks at a time.

14th July 1983

Four days of sheer hell and boredom. Today, thank heavens, we are back to normal. The trade winds and whistling jack are in harmony and the mood of the crew is optimistic.

15h00: Wind gusting 30 knots. Suddenly the jib sail flaps helplessly in the stiff breeze. The baby stay has snapped at the bow. All hands on deck to haul down the main sheet and the spinnaker. This set back is nothing new for our skipper. With the help of Gary and Graham, Andy manufactures a jury rig (a temporary repair). With a sense of urgency, searching in the bosun's locker for spare steel cable, turnkeys and fittings to get underway without further delay. Black Jed is drifting helplessly every which way in the metre high swells.

Debbie on the lookout calls excitedly to all and sundry and points dead ahead. A big black hump on the horizon. Twenty tons of blubber is bearing down on us. Now Debbie is hysterically screaming, Whale! Whale! This tremendous mammal is swaying and heaving silently through the water. It passes us majestically, not more than twenty metres on the starboard side of our delicate vessel. A fountain of water spouting from his blow hole. Looking straight ahead, he is seemingly oblivious of our very existence. It was easily twice the length of our yacht and dwarfed us like a nuclear submarine. Intimidating!

Gary declares this to be a blue whale, the largest of the species. Mature animals grow to a length of 30 metres or more. I can still see this behemoth in my mind's eye. It is one of the most feared objects by yachtsman. A collision with one of these at sea is not uncommon. It happens so suddenly and many a crew, in the twinkling of an eye, are left floundering with splintered fiberglass all around them. No time to don life jackets or launch a life raft or transmit a distress signal.

On hindsight, it could have been providence that our baby stay gave up just minutes before, at that particular time and place? Someone was looking after us!

15th July 1983

04H00: Blinking through the mist and first light of dawn is the faint glow from the mainland of Portugal. Andy calls for our handheld radar/Morse identification scope. Me, being the "official" radio operator, points the contraption in the general direction of the land signal, and the Morse code comes through. "Dah dit dah dit. Dit dit. Dit dit day. I translate for Andy. C. S. V. The abbreviation for Cape St. Vincent. Andy's navigation is again spot-on. Champagne breakfast coming up.

We now change course to 110 degrees. The craggy Portuguese coastline on our port side. A beautiful day. Black Jed weaving slowly in between small rocky outcrops of uninhabited islets. The coast looks very forbidding and barren, as if the whole country is in the throes of a drought. Much as I imagine the landscape of the moon to look like.

12h00: After 4 hours of motoring there is a sudden sharp change in the character of the coast line. The famous Algarve comes up on the map. Everything is green. Small holdings with quaint houses, pastures with grazing cows and goats. Palm trees in abundance. Many luxury homes on the coast line with their own private jetties. Then a country club with luxuriant and immaculate fairways and greens. A millionaire only golf club. We are so close to the shore we can see golfers teeing up.

We are not seen by the wind surfers and kids sailing small dabchicks. Excitedly sailing and skimming dangerously across our track. We ask if anybody speaks English and many voices reply in the affirmative.

The Algarve is a favourite destination of the British. "How far to Villamoura" we ask. "Keep going, another 5 kilometres and you're there". The name Villamoura translates to Village of the Moors. Centuries before, Portugal was under domination of the Turks, hence the moniker.

15h00: Into the welcome bosom of Marina Villamoura. A modern yacht terminal, designed by experts, for the handling and mooring expeditiously of visiting mariners from all over the world. A reception committee allocates a berth according to type and size. Board walks and anchorage points in abundance. Gingerly, with utmost care, we idle in to our appointed berth. Don't want to rupture the hull at this stage!

We stare in wonderment at the high-rise holiday apartment blocks and the most beautiful and sleek yachts and motor cruisers that are in abundance in the Marina. Shades of Donald Trump and Aristotle Onassis. Luxury, opulence and extravagance all around. Thousands of tourists, suitably attired for the holiday scene and climate are strolling around ogling each other and the myriad of craft, ranging from catamarans, ketches, sloops, skiffs, and motor sailboats, from distant, exotic places.

A few minutes away there is a shopping mall with hundreds of small specialist shops, supermarkets, travel agents, hair dressers. All catering for those travelling steerage to a notch higher than first class.

3 months at sea had left us in not the most elegant state to receive visitors. Still, there were many curios passersby gaping and gawking at us. It was nice to be the centre of attention. We did feel a little like extra-terrestrials from outer space.

From cramped quarters, rationed water and diesel fuel, beery bread and living in each other's pockets we are suddenly out of jail. The transition is not easy to get accustomed to.

I now have two priorities. The first, a visit to a tonsorial expert and the luxury of a haircut, manicure and the removal of three months of swarthy beard. Next, a visit to the travel agent for two tickets. A bus ride to Lisbon and an airfare to London.

14 CHANCE ENCOUNTERS

Back home in the Free State where I live, a number of farms and villages were named by expatriate Scots who served in the British Forces during the Boer War. My farm is called Loch Katrine and is situated on the banks of Loch Lomond. Some years after buying the farm I came across a print of an old masterpiece, titled "Loch Katrine at Sunrise" by H. R. Hall. This picture hangs in my lounge and depicts a mystical and misty scene of the loch, with craggy pastured hills rising from the edge of the waters and long horned highland cattle grazing. I always vowed to myself that one day I would visit the real Loch Katrine in Scotland.

On landing at Heathrow, I cleared customs and took the underground in to central London. I was going to make good on the promise to myself to visit the famous Loch Katrine.

In addition, after an arduous three month trip, coupled up with six other individuals, no privacy and aware of the ever threat of danger haunting our every waking moment the thought of spending an idyllic week of rest and recuperation was heaven.

The Visitor's Bureau advised me to make Glasgow my next port of call, being the central jumping off point for visiting Loch country. At Euston station I boarded the "Flying Scotsman". This is a pleasant, all day, train trip through the beautiful English countryside and into the grimy heart of Glasgow.

Another country and another language! I found inordinate difficulty in understanding and attuning my ear to the broad Scots brogue. As witness to my predicament, when I paid a visit to the Visitors Bureau. The conversation went something like this:

"Gud morrrrning sur. Can I be of hulp" said a sweet young Scots lass behind the counter.

"Yes please. Can you advise me how to get to Loch Katreena?" I replied in my South African accent.

She looked at me in bewilderment, advising me that she did not know of such a place. I insisted that there must be, after all I had just sailed half way round the world to visit it. She then turned to one of her young colleagues, enquiring if she knew of a place called Loch Katreena. Again, consternation reigned supreme. Out came a large map and curly heads bent over a spider web of Scottish lanes, roads, lochs, rivers and railway lines. "Sorry sur, nay setch a ples".

Despondently I took my leave. Half way up the block I suddenly feel a tug at my sleeve. The young office boy from the bureau was at my side.

"Came back sur, the munnuger wishes to speak wi you".

He had heard my conversation with the two lasses and, on cogitating about my request suddenly came to the realization that what I was looking for was "Loch Katrin". Another pronunciation of Loch Katrine.

Scanning the map once more "Laddie, your needing a nose a sharrrp as a peen to unurrth this wee loch".

I noted carefully the instructions to get to this elusive loch. Take a bus to Aberfoyle. Sleep there overnight and then take a taxi to Loch Katrine. No trains or public transport.

I had some time before the bus would leave Glasgow, so I spent some time strolling along in the busy shopping centre. I found a shopping mall with dozens of small and large specialist shops catering for all types of merchandise. I popped into an emporium similar to our huge hypermarkets. Aisles and aisles of huge quantities of electrical appliances, sporting goods, bedding, linen, furniture, TV, radios, and stereo equipment.

Whilst wandering around like a lost soul, this young congenial woman, with a friendly countenance approached me.

"Good morning" she greets me, "can I help you?"

"No thanks, to be truthful, I'm just browsing, killing time", I reply.

"You sound like a South African?" she says.

"As a matter of fact, I am."

"What part of South Africa are you from?"

"I don't know if you are familiar with South Africa, but I come from the Orange Free State."

"The Free State, What town?"

"It's just a small obscure place, hardly on the map."

"Tell me, I'm interested to know."

"Well, it's a small town called Bethlehem."

"Bethlehem! I know Bethlehem. "

"What do you mean, you know Bethlehem?"

"I lived there for many years and went to school there."

"That's interesting. How long ago?"

"As a baby at the age of 3 weeks, I went to live with my grandparents and completed my schooling there."

"What did your grandfather do for a living?"

"He was the accountant with a firm of merchant wholesalers."

At this stage I am beginning to look at her in amazement.

"What was the name of this company?" I asked.

"Swartzberg Wholesalers, and my grandfather was Sidney Holcombe."

I am dumbstruck. The little wheels in my head start cartwheeling. Thinking back to the days, as a teenager, when I helped my Dad after school, and subsequently worked full time with him from 1949, after serving in the Israeli Air Force. I recall a little toddler, coming in to the warehouse, bringing her grandfather a flask of tea and sandwiches.

I exclaim; "You must be Noreen."

She replies, hardly containing herself; "And you must be Zan. Don't you remember me as a teenager, making a nuisance of myself and you told me to go away and grow up? Well, I got married, came to Scotland and now, twenty-six years later, I have grown up."

Our lives seemed to have run in parallel paths since those early Bethlehem days. We both got married around the same time, we both got divorced in the same year.

I still find it incredible and often ask myself if fate, or my guardian angel was working hard over the years. Some imponderables:

Why did I buy a farm with the most unusual name of "Loch Katrine"? Why did I buy, from an out of the way antique shop, the picture "Loch Katrine Sunset"? Who imported this picture into the country and why? Why was I irrevocably drawn to visit this place in Scotland? How is that the Manager at the Visitors Bureau just happened to hear the conversation and call me back, with the result I had four hours to spare. Why did this shop assistant approach me?

Taking all these factors into consideration it is surely a trillion to one chance of such a happenstance.

The story didn't end there. On 2nd June 1989 Noreen and I were married.

IN MEMORIAM

Stephen Sykes
1961 – 1984

Stephen joined Black Jed in East London and crewed with us to our destination in Villamoura, Portugal. He was a wonderful young man, enthusiastic, good natured and extremely good looking, with sun bleached blonde hair. I found him to be always respectful and ready to lend a hand, no matter if it was for the most menial tasks.

He was born with "sea water in his veins". A talent with the needle at repairing sails and cooking up a delicious meal in the cramped confines of a yacht galley.

Strangely, during our trip on Black Jet, I took more photographs of Stephen than any other crewman.

In what is considered one of South Africa's worst yachting tragedies, Stephen was lost while crewing yacht Rubicon in the Wilbur Ellis da Gama yacht race from Durban to East London in 1984.

The yacht was sailing in winds of up to 100km/hour in waves 10 metre high. The yacht and the five man crew, including a young reporter from the Cape Times who was reporting the race and was on board a yacht for the first time, was last seen off the Wild Coast.

Extensive searches were conducted but nothing was found; no wreckage, no debris, no bodies and no clue of what could have happened to it.

In 2014, I visited the Royal Durban Yacht Club on a happenchance visit. They were holding a commemorative display for those lost during this race in 1984, 30 years earlier. In the entrance was a report of the tragedy. I asked the secretary if she would like a picture of Stephen. They were delighted to receive one from me. The display brought back many memories of this fine young man.

A Young Reporter
? – 1984

Her first time on a yacht, she was reporting on the race and sadly lost her life when Yacht Rubicon went down.

GALLERY

A selection of photographs from my private collection.

Yacht Black Jed

Yacht Black Jed at Royal Cape Yacht Club

Stephen and Zan provisioning at The Royal Cape Yacht Club

Crew Shirts from Taffy. Now which way?

Andy and Gary in the cockpit

This is Sailing

Zan, Relaxing on board.

Relaxing in the Sun and Paul with our dinner – Yellow Fin Tuna

Who's in Charge? Zan and Graham

Zan helming

Main Sail pulling along nicely.

Spinnaker

Arrival in St Helena

Sheralee at the 999 Steps in St Helena.

Werner freeing the anchor at St Helena and we are on our way.

Graveyard in Ascension Island

Zan sightseeing.

A round of golf at the Ascension Island Golf Club.

Farewell Ascension – Fly-by from RAF.

Sun Setting

Arriving in Horta, Azores Islands

Having fun in the Rubber Dinghy

Tied up in Harbour and Departing Ponta Delgado, Azores

Arrival in Villamoura, Portugal

The Crew - Zan, Sheralee, Graham, Debbie, Andy, Gary

www.ingramcontent.com/pod-product-compliance
Lightning Source LLC
LaVergne TN
LVHW010033070426
835509LV00004B/138